The
ESSENTIAL
Dog Owner's
GUIDE

Creative Direction: Saeah Wood

Production & Editorial Management: Amy Reed

Editorial: Kendra Muntz, Amy Reed, & Christa Evans

Design: Ivica Jandrijević

Production & Editorial Assistance: Charlie, Ullr, & Sophie

Illustrations: @Fantuzura

ISBN:
Paperback: 978-1-955671-37-8
E-Book: 978-1-955671-38-5

essentialdogownersguide.com

Printed in the United States of America

otterpine.com

The
ESSENTIAL
Dog Owner's
GUIDE

A Reference for the Responsible Dog Owner

EVAN MILNOR & M. REED MILNOR

DEDICATED TO:

Charlie Gunner, Ullr Olaf, and Sophie Odelette

Thank you for inspiring this book.

You make life better.
We hope we do the same for you.

SPECIAL THANKS

Our most heartfelt thanks to everyone who supported the writing of this book—it would not have been possible without your feedback and expert advice. Thank you to Dr. Steve Pope, DVM, and Kim Pope: your generosity in time, expertise, and encouragement during the research and writing process was invaluable. Thank you to Dr. Maritza Perez-Bruno, DVM, for your wonderfully insightful feedback on the manuscript. To our incredible editor Kendra Muntz: without your expert guidance, keen attention to detail, and passion for this project, we could not have pulled this off. To the Otterpine team, with special gratitude to Saeah Wood and Amy Reed, for embarking on this project and transforming our vision into a reality that has far exceeded our expectations—your incredible work has left us in awe. To Dr. Erin Collner, DVM, Dr. Kelly Jones, DVM, Dr. Suzanne Ford, DVM, and the dozens of shelter owners and breeders who we surveyed at the early stages of the writing process: your insights were immeasurably helpful in defining the direction of this book. And of course, thank you to our loving family who supported and encouraged the pursuit of this project.

CONTENTS

CHAPTER TWO

PREPARING FOR YOUR NEW FAMILY MEMBER

CHAPTER THREE

RESPONSIBLE DOG PARENTING

CHAPTER FOUR

RESOURCES AND FURTHER READING

PREFACE

Today, dogs are the best friend of humankind the world over. Dogs are by our side through every life event—births, deaths, and all of the joyous and sorrowful moments in between. But how did these compassionate animals become such trusted companions?

About 14,000 years ago, likely somewhere in the northern tundra of Eurasia, an intrepid wolf may have approached the camp of primitive men to find a few scraps of leftover food. Or perhaps somewhere else in that same desolate wilderness, a member of a tribal hunting party came across an abandoned litter of wolf pups and, seeing them without their mother, took pity and brought them back to camp to nurture and raise as members of the tribe.

While we will never know details about the exact encounter, we do know that early man saw something different in wolves from other animals, perhaps an empathetic connection with the shared struggle for survival. Recognizing that a better existence could be found through cooperation rather than competition, man and wolf formed an early mutual relationship. Over generations, the mutual trust grew and the symbiotic relationship evolved between humans and wolves. Wolves were domesticated and bred for various functions based on their unique traits, paving the way to the hundreds of different breeds of modern dogs we know today.

Now, millions of people around the world enjoy the companionship of dogs in all aspects of daily life. Dogs parachute with their trainers into combat zones, provide friendship for seniors, guide the physically impaired, detect medical conditions with their highly attuned sense of smell, and provide endless joy for their human owners. It is therefore imperative that we offer our dogs the same love, support, and respect that they show us every day.

As you consider bringing a new dog into your life, you are continuing this ancient relationship—one built on mutual trust, interdependence, and unconditional love. As you make this important decision, we hope this guidebook will serve as an easy-to-use, invaluable resource about the fundamentals of dog ownership. Assembled from a wide variety of sources and experts, this guide provides a brief overview of some of the most essential and practical information a family should know before becoming dog owners. Whether you are a first-time or experienced dog owner, our goal is to help equip you with the knowledge and resources you need to create a successful relationship with your pup.

Thank you for joining us!

SHOULD I GET A DOG?

*Dogs are our link to paradise. They don't
know evil or jealousy or discontent. To
sit with a dog on a hillside on a glorious
afternoon is to be back in Eden, where doing
nothing was not boring—it was peace.*

— MILAN KUNDERA

As you make the decision to bring a dog into your family, the continuation of the age-old trusted relationship between dogs and humans will be carried forth through your actions. Your dog's behavior and happiness in life will ultimately be a direct result of the time and attention you invest in the relationship.

Along with selecting a spouse, having children, and deciding on a career, bringing a dog into the family is one of the most significant and meaningful choices a person can make. Dogs can bring a family happiness, unconditional love, and affection. By learning how to provide a good life for them, they, in turn, teach us how to be better humans and lead more joyful and fulfilling lives.

Dogs, however, will also introduce significant new responsibilities, substantial time and energy commitments, occasional frustrations, and financial considerations into your life that are not to be taken lightly. You may not be ready to bring a new dog into your home without first weighing the challenges and responsibilities as heavily as the many positive factors. A dog is a lot of work—and work is required every single day.

If your professional or personal commitments are likely to keep you away from home for long periods of time or prevent you from devoting sufficient care and attention to your dog, consider waiting for a better time to own a dog. Just like children, all dogs deserve parents who are responsible and prepared to dedicate sufficient love, time, care, attention, and resources to raise them properly. If you are unsure about your willingness or ability to make this ongoing commitment in the years ahead, then now is likely not the ideal time for your family to adopt.

If, however, you decide you are ready to take the leap, we hope you find this book helpful, and we welcome you with enthusiasm to the worldwide community of dog owners.

CHAPTER ONE

DECIDING ON A DOG

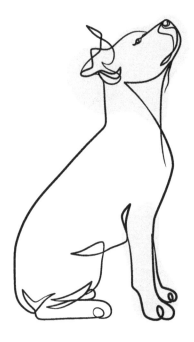

"Everyone thinks they have the best dog, and none of them are wrong."

— W. R. PURSCHE

SELECTING A BREED

So, you have decided to bring a new dog into the family. Congratulations! One of the first factors you may consider when deciding upon a dog is what breed or type is best for your family. When studying dog types, be sure to thoroughly research the breed, including the expected adult size and weight, life expectancy, temperament, and specific trends for that breed at various ages. You should understand how the dog will likely age, grow, and behave from puppyhood through adolescence and adulthood to old age, including the likelihood of various health conditions and behavioral patterns common to the breed.

To find the ideal dog for you and your family, take into account how all of the breed-specific criteria may or may not match with your lifestyle and living space. For example, a breed that will grow to be large and require a lot of space to move around will likely be better suited for a home with a yard rather than a small apartment. A high-energy dog that requires a great deal of exercise might not be an ideal fit for an individual less willing or able to exercise their dog daily. Identifying criteria such as these is critical to ensuring that your family and your dog will thrive together.

It is also important to know whether members of your family have allergic reactions to dogs. Although no dog is "nonallergenic," some breeds are more hypoallergenic than others, meaning that they cause less severe allergic reactions in humans than do other breeds. This health condition may be important to consider as you select your ideal canine companion.

An excellent resource for learning more about different breeds and comparing their tendencies is the American Kennel Club (AKC). The AKC is the gold standard in the US for dog breed classification, training guidance, health information, and research-based dog expertise.

Dogs adopted from shelters, however, are often a mix of two or more different breeds, and the exact breed combination may not be known. Mixed-breed dogs have combinations of features and temperaments that make each dog unique and special, though less easily predicted. To ensure that a mixed-breed dog will be a good fit for your family, spend as much time with the dog as possible at the shelter or rescue organization before adoption to understand their behavioral tendencies.

To help you decide which type of dog will be ideal for your family's needs, reference the following quick guide on various dog groups and functions.

Dog Groups

The AKC categorizes dog breeds into the following seven major groups based on the function the dogs were originally bred to perform:

- **WORKING:** These dogs are categorized by their labor-intensive tasks such as sled pulling and protection. As their name says, these are the workers of the dog kingdom, and they are often determined, high-energy, and physically strong. Examples include Boxers, Great Danes, Siberian Huskies, and Samoyeds.

- **HERDING:** These dogs were bred to efficiently herd, move, and contain such livestock as sheep, cattle, and reindeer. They tend to be high-energy, intelligent, extremely loyal, and task oriented. Examples include Border Collies, German Shepherds, and Welsh Corgis.

- **TOY:** These dogs were bred to be close, affectionate, and loyal home companions. Their small size makes them a good choice for city or apartment dwellers. Examples include Chihuahuas, Pugs, and Shih Tzus.

- **HOUND:** These dogs were bred to track warm-blooded prey like rabbits, raccoons, foxes, and deer. Sighthounds rely on their vision and impressive speed, while scenthounds depend on their strong sense of smell to track prey. Examples include Beagles, Greyhounds, and Bloodhounds.

- **SPORTING:** These dogs were bred to support hunters in capturing and retrieving feathered game. They commonly have thick, water-repellent coats. Examples include Golden and Labrador Retrievers, Irish Setters, Vizslas, and Cocker Spaniels.

- **TERRIER:** These breeds specialize in pursuing rodents and underground crop-harming vermin. Depending on the length of their legs, breeds of this group attack pests using different approaches. Examples include Jack Russell Terriers, Miniature Schnauzers, and Yorkshire Terriers.

● **NON-SPORTING:** This group is a miscellaneous collection of breeds that do not fall specifically into any of the other categories. Although they do not have a specific sporting function, they were bred for human companionship. Examples include Boston Terriers, Bulldogs, Poodles, and Dalmatians.

SERVICE, THERAPY, EMOTIONAL SUPPORT, AND WORKING DOGS

Though this book focuses on dogs as household companions, dogs can also serve a number of critical service and working functions. The following four groups distinguish among canines that are trained to perform support tasks for their human companions.

Service Dogs

Service dogs are specially trained to perform tasks related to the health and safety of people with disabilities. The Americans with Disabilities Act (ADA) regulates the use of service dogs and defines a disability as "a physical or mental impairment that substantially limits one or more major life activities." The duties performed by service dogs range widely and include guide functions to assist the visually impaired, detection and mitigation of mental or physical health episodes such as panic attacks, seizures, or post-traumatic stress disorder, and other vital tasks. Official service dogs are legally permitted to enter premises where dogs are otherwise prohibited. The ADA website, US Service Animal Registrar, and the American Kennel Club are great resources for more information on qualified disabilities and guidance on how to find or train a service dog.

Therapy Dogs

Therapy dogs are not classified as official service dogs and do not receive the same access privileges. Volunteer organizations use therapy dogs to provide emotional comfort to people in stressful settings where psychological support is welcome, including hospitals, assisted living homes, disaster sites, and courthouses.

Emotional Support Dogs

Emotional support animals (ESAs) are not classified as official service dogs. At times, these dogs may be allowed to accompany owners in public places where dogs are otherwise prohibited, but they are not granted the same unlimited access as service dogs. Though they may be trained to provide emotional support to an owner with a mental health condition, ESAs solely provide companionship and are not trained to perform specific duties.

Working Dogs

Working dogs are trained to assist with professional occupations to augment human capabilities. These dogs use their highly attuned sense of smell, hearing, and other sensory inputs to detect the world in ways that humans cannot. Examples of working dogs include explosives and drug detection dogs used by law enforcement, search and rescue dogs used by disaster response teams, military working dogs used for a variety of combat support functions, and cancer and allergen detection dogs.

If you are considering owning a dog for a service or working function, it is important to consult with expert trainers familiar with the specific training requirements and certifications. These experts can help you find, evaluate, train, or qualify a dog to meet specific needs. See Appendix A: Additional Resources for more information about service dog training and certification.

THE SEARCH

Once you determine the type of dog that is best for you, another key factor is whether to adopt a dog from a rescue shelter or "shop" for a new dog through breeders. Of course, you may also find yourself unexpectedly adopting a dog—either by finding and falling in love with a stray, or by meeting a dog at an adoption event or rescue shelter that seems like a good fit. Regardless of the circumstances, the guidance in this chapter will help you through this decision-making process.

If you are choosing between adopting through a shelter or finding a breeder, here are some important pros and cons to consider for each option.

ADOPTION PROS AND CONS

PROS

+ About three to four million dogs are euthanized annually due to lack of space and resources at rescue facilities. By adopting, you can save the life of two dogs—the one you adopt and the one your dog makes space for at the shelter who now has a chance to find a forever home.

+ Adoption is often less expensive. Dogs from breeders can cost thousands of dollars. Adoption fees from shelters can range from $50 to $300+, and shelters typically ensure their dogs are spayed or neutered, microchipped, dewormed, and vaccinated, saving hundreds of dollars more in veterinary fees.

+ Mixed breeds are more likely to be found at shelters. They may be healthier and have fewer health and genetic complications than purebreds.

+ Shelter dogs are typically adolescents or adults and may already be partially or fully responsive to commands, housebroken, trained, and/or socialized. Puppies require a lot more time, training, cost, and attention!

- Many shelters will help an adopting family find a dog with an ideal temperament for their home to ensure a good fit. Although disruptive to the dog's transition in the short term, many shelters will allow you a several-week trial period during which you can bring a newly adopted dog back to the shelter if the adoption does not work out for your family. Common reasons for returning a dog during this period include identification of behaviors that are incompatible with the adopting family and discovery of an existing health condition during an initial veterinary visit that the adopting family is not prepared to face.

- Fostering is when a person takes a dog from a rescue or shelter and cares for it in their home temporarily. This arrangement can be a great option to test the waters and transition gradually into dog ownership, while at the same time helping a dog in their journey to find a forever home.

CONS

- By adopting, you cannot as easily select for age, pure breeding, disposition, or background. Many sites, however, such as www.adoptapet.com and www.petfinder.com, allow you to set search criteria and receive notifications when your ideal breed or type needs adoption. Nonetheless, adoption organizations often will not know the history or exact breed of a dog, making it harder to predict its temperament and behavioral tendencies.

- Typically, shelters will house adolescent or adult dogs rather than puppies, which may discourage a family from adopting if they wish to raise a dog for its entire life.

- In general, although mixed-breed dogs tend to have fewer health concerns, these concerns are less predictable than those in purebred dogs.

- While most dogs arrive in shelters due to challenging circumstances (e.g., divorce, financial constraints, moving, or lack of time), the dog also may have been poorly socialized or abused, which can be difficult for an adopting family to quickly assess. Shelter dogs may have anxiety from loneliness and isolation, possessiveness from competing with other dogs for food or toys, aggressive tendencies, or unknown behavior triggers. Before adopting, be sure to plan multiple visits to the shelter with all members of the family at different times of day to ensure there are no disqualifying behavioral concerns. See Appendix B: Temperament Assessment for a list of questions to ask and methods of evaluating a shelter dog's temperament before adoption.

BREEDER PROS AND CONS

PROS

⊕ Finding a dog through a breeder enables you to select a specific breed with known characteristics. Quality breeders devote their lives to improving the breed and health of their dogs rather than making money. Good breeders focus on how well their dogs represent the breed rather than the quantity of puppies they can breed and sell. In addition, many quality breeders show their own dogs in competitions. Use authoritative references and resources such as the AKC breeder search to find reputable, licensed breeders in your area. Although AKC breeding recognition is a good start, be diligent in researching each breeder's dedication to canine health. Many breeders will strive to attain health condition certifications. For example, if a breed is predisposed to hip dysplasia, a breeder may have a certification stating that they specifically breed their dogs to minimize the likelihood of this condition.

⊕ Breeders will know the social, health, and genetic background of their dogs. Most breeders sell puppies rather than adult dogs and will allow adopting families to see the dog parents and meet the litter.

Once the puppies are about 6–7 weeks old, families can bring the new dog home and raise it from puppy stages through adulthood.

⊕ You may need to use a breeder if you are looking for a dog to serve a specific function or activity. Certain breeders specialize in breeding their dogs based on a functional group or purpose (e.g., hunting, therapy, working, service, competitions, or sports).

CONS

⊖ It is important to ensure you are working with a reputable breeder to avoid supporting "puppy mills." Puppy mills are factory-style breeding facilities that are purely motivated by profit. These organizations often sell animals through pet stores or online ads and may engage in unethical practices. Additionally, be sure to avoid amateur "backyard breeders" who are likely unaware of the genetic implications of their breeding decisions and are often not equipped for responsibly breeding and socializing large numbers of dogs. Purchasing from these vendors incentivizes more breeding when there are many dogs already in need of adoption at shelters who could end up euthanized.

⊖ Purchasing a dog through a breeder is often more expensive both in up-front costs (from $500 to $2,000+) and ongoing costs for training, veterinary visits, and medical procedures such as spaying/neutering and microchipping. By purchasing a puppy, you are committing to more time, attention, and expenses than you would by adopting an adult dog.

- Breeders may not offer the same support structure that rescue shelters often provide, such as partnerships or discounts with veterinary hospitals, daycare programs, boarding centers, trainers, or community groups. Look for a breeder whose mission is to ensure that their dogs end up in healthy, happy homes.

BUDGETING

Regardless of which breed you select and whether you find your ideal dog at a shelter or breeder, it is important to weigh the financial implications of dog ownership. Dogs can be expensive, and many new dog owners vastly underestimate the costs they will incur. See Appendix C: Budgeting Worksheet for a helpful tool to plan for expenses. Here are some key things to consider regarding the costs of dog ownership.

Up-Front Costs

- Bringing home a new dog tends to require a disproportionate amount of expenses up front, and costs will begin to taper off and normalize once you establish a routine.

- Plan to budget anywhere from $500 to $2,000+ for adoption or breeder fees plus initial supplies. See Chapter 2: Preparing for Your New Family Member for more guidance.

- Budget another $500 to $2,000 per year for food, supplies, vet visits, medications, treats, grooming, toys, etc.

- Costs can vary widely depending on medical needs, food choice, toys, crate, bed, stroller, gating or fence installation, house preparations, and other supplies.

Ongoing Costs

➡ Once you purchase the essentials, costs will likely stabilize. Food, veterinary visits, daycare, and boarding are the most consistent ongoing expenses.

➡ Reoccurring pet food delivery services, like Amazon's Subscribe and Save, are an affordable and convenient way to ensure your preferred food is in stock at a good price. See the Diet section in chapter 3 for more about feeding your dog.

➡ Apartment complexes, landlords, and living communities often have guidelines pertaining to pets living on premises. They may have dog breed or size restrictions and are likely to impose a one-time and/or recurring fee for pet owners. These fees may range from $50 to $120+ per month for cleaning and other expenses.

Emergency Expenses

➡ If feasible, set aside a small monthly amount into an emergency fund to help pay for surprise expenses like medical bills, boarding, etc.

➡ Dog owners are likely to incur at least one $2,000 to $4,000+ emergency medical care or chronic health condition expense during their pet's lifetime.

Insurance

- If you are concerned about your ability to cover surprise expenses out of pocket, research pet insurance options. Note that many insurers will still require you to pay vet hospital bills directly out of pocket and then file claims for reimbursement.

- Lemonade, Eusoh (Community Health), CareCredit, and other innovative options now exist to help diffuse the cost of pet care. Plans can start as low as $10 per month. Some companies also offer lines of credit for large emergency pet expenses.

- Use insurance comparison websites to find a plan that is appropriate for your situation. Policies vary in the type of coverage they provide and may have specific exclusions, especially on preexisting health conditions, dental coverage, and other routine treatments (e.g., anal gland expression and nail trims). Some companies do not cover certain dog breeds that they find to be aggressive and prone to injury. Other insurance providers may provide coverage only at particular animal hospitals under the terms of the policy. Be sure to do ample research to find the policy that is right for you.

CHAPTER TWO

PREPARING FOR YOUR NEW FAMILY MEMBER

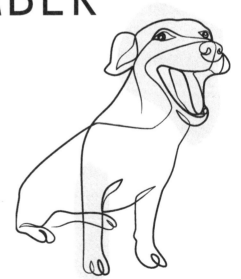

A house is not a home until it has a dog.

— GERALD DURRELL

PREPARING THE HOUSE

It is important to properly prepare your home before you welcome your new dog. Consider your living space as well as how you would like your dog to interact with each member of the family. Be sure that every family member is aligned on expectations, division of care responsibilities, commands, and training styles before the dog is brought into the new home (see the Training and Behavior section in chapter 3 for more guidance). Establish a consistent schedule for walking, feeding, going potty, playing, and sleeping so your dog can establish a new routine.

Key Preparations

The first preparation you will need to make is deciding on a veterinarian. See the Selecting a Veterinarian section in chapter 3 for more guidance.

Once you select a veterinarian that meets your needs, be sure that the vet's contact information and poison control numbers are visibly posted on the refrigerator or another common area. See Appendix D: Contact Information to help keep this information organized and accessible. Also see Appendix E: Pet Alert for a sample decal to place on your front door to alert emergency responders to the presence of pets in the residence.

Start a consolidated file for medical records and other documentation and store it in a safe place that everyone in the family can access and reference as needed.

Be sure to schedule an initial veterinary checkup within the first two weeks of bringing your dog home. It is often best to wait until your dog has settled in for a few days before bringing them to their first vet visit.

Make sure to have all necessary supplies on hand, as discussed in the next section.

Dog-Proofing

All dogs will behave in their own unique way in their new home. Walk through each room and dog-proof your home, making sure any potentially hazardous, breakable, or chewable items (like children's toys, electrical cords, chemicals, food, pillows, plants, shoes, etc.) are locked away, gated off, or placed high enough that they cannot be reached. Be aware that countertops may not be out of reach of a curious and determined dog.

Gating the House

Once you grant your dog access to a certain portion of the house, it will become difficult to reclaim that space in the future. Whether a bedroom, living room, or expensive couch, if you want to restrict access to a portion of the house, gate off the area before bringing the dog home, and do not introduce it to the dog at all. Be aware that dark, secluded areas or rooms that are not often used (especially carpeted areas) are likely places for potty accidents.

Shedding Control and Cleaning Supplies

Many dog breeds will shed hair throughout the house on fabrics, carpets, and clothing. They will occasionally create a mess. Owning a good vacuum, pet-friendly cleaning supplies, and dedicated towels to wipe off your dog after walk on rainy or muddy days are a must.

Look for household cleaning supplies that are nontoxic and pet safe to avoid introducing chemicals onto floors and surfaces that could pose a risk to your dog.

SHELTER

Just as humans need a sense of place to feel comfortable and safe, dogs also benefit from developing familiarity with the locations where they will be spending much of their time. Consider each of these environments and how to make them conducive to your dog's needs.

Crate

A sturdy crate can be a great tool for providing your dog with a safe and secluded space and can help you keep your dog in a controlled environment during unsupervised time. However, crate usage should be approached thoughtfully to ensure that your dog builds a positive association with the space and can still spend most of the time in more open, social environments.

Find a crate that is large enough for your dog to comfortably stand up and turn around, but not so big that there is a lot of extra space. Some crates have adjustable or removable dividers to expand the same crate as your dog grows. Purchasing a pad or bed for the bottom of the crate can make it a more comfortable place to sleep. Find a designated, cleanable spot in the house for your dog's crate that can be used as their special sanctuary.

Dogs like to sleep in cave-like environments with overhead cover. In time, your dog's crate should become a comfortable sanctuary, even if they are initially anxious to use it. Research common crate-training techniques and watch online videos on how to gradually approach this learning curve with patience so your dog will build a positive rather than negative association with the crate.

Dog Carrier

For smaller dogs, you may also want to purchase a travel-friendly dog carrier suitable for car rides or airplanes. Many of these carriers are collapsible and lightweight, allowing for easy transport and storage.

Bed

Dogs tend to sleep an average of 12–14 hours per day, so picking a comfortable bed for your dog is important. However, your dog will likely sleep in various favorite spots in the home and may not fully embrace their designated bed. Observe your dog's preferences over time to inform your choice of bed.

The Yard

Dogs are bred and socialized specifically for human companionship, so while most dogs love going outside, they should generally live indoors among human companions. It is important, though, to identify a suitable outdoor space where you can take your dog to exercise, potty, and play. Depending on your living situation, this may be your own yard, a local dog run, a nearby public grassy area, or a park designated for dogs.

When possible, a fenced-in yard is a great option to allow your dog to roam freely while staying safe and out of trouble. However, a determined and agile dog can find a way over, under, or through even a seemingly high and sturdy fence. Consider installing a privacy fence so your dog will not be tormented by the sight of passersby or wildlife that are out of reach. Electric dog fences, while often effective, may not be enough to contain a strong-willed dog chasing after something beyond the border. Some electric fences may also deliver a shock on re-entry to the perimeter, deterring your dog from returning home.

Physical barriers are generally best when possible. If you use a stake in the ground with a cable tie-out or aerial runner to keep your dog in the yard, be sure to maintain supervision, as dogs can become tangled in the cables or ropes. Access to a yard environment is not a substitute for regular walks and exercise.

Backyard Blues

If you leave your dog outdoors for an extended period of time, ensure they have access to enough food and water, cannot reach hazardous items or areas, and are not exposed to dangerous weather conditions that could lead to overheating or frostbite. Since they are bred to cohabitate with humans, dogs left outdoors and unattended for too long can become poorly socialized, anxious, or depressed.

Initial Welcome

Plan to devote at least the first full day to acquaint your dog with its new home. Give them plenty of attention while also granting enough space for them to explore the house and not feel overwhelmed.

When you first bring your dog into your home, immediately show your pup where to go potty, whether in the yard or on training papers (see the Potty Training section in chapter 3 for more guidance). Let them sniff around the area freely. The first several times they potty in the proper place, strongly reinforce the behavior by extravagantly praising them and rewarding with treats.

3/3/3 Rule

A good rule of thumb when adopting a new dog is the three day, three week, three month rule. After bringing home your new dog, you are likely to see a distinct change in behavioral patterns at approximately these intervals, though each dog is different and will acclimate on a unique timeline.

THREE DAYS: During the first three days, your dog is likely anxious and overwhelmed, unsure of what to expect in the new environment. They may self-isolate, test boundaries, have potty accidents, or exhibit unusual eating or drinking behaviors, including not eating or drinking at all. Remain calm and positive, stick to a routine as much as possible, and recognize that this behavior will likely change soon.

THREE WEEKS: After a few weeks your dog will begin to settle into the new routine, learn the environment, and gradually build trust with the new family. At this point, your dog may begin to let their guard down and show their true personality, including potentially starting to exhibit some of the behavioral issues listed in the Behavioral Problems and Expectations section in chapter 3.

THREE MONTHS: After three months, your dog will likely feel completely comfortable in their new home. They will have established trust and security with their family and will become even more set in their routine, showing affection and often demonstrating good habits. Continuous training is still critical, but affection and trust can be powerful tools to reinforce positive behaviors.

CHAPTER THREE

RESPONSIBLE DOG PARENTING

If you think dogs can't count, try putting three dog biscuits in your pocket and then give him only two of them.

—PHIL PASTORET

MEDICAL

The first step to responsible dog parenting is keeping your dog physically healthy. This process starts with finding the right veterinarian.

Selecting a Veterinarian

While searching for your dog's veterinarian, think about the aspects you like about your own doctor, including:

● ACCESSIBILITY AND DISTANCE FROM HOME

Know the location and hours of operation of your general practice veterinary clinic. Keep the phone number and address of your primary veterinarian as well as a 24-hour veterinary hospital easily accessible in case of an emergency for when your primary veterinary office is closed. See Appendix D: Contact Information for quick reference.

In general, services, diagnostics, and medications are significantly more expensive when purchased at emergency veterinary hospitals than at your general practice clinic.

● RESPONSIVENESS

Most veterinarians have a very heavy caseload. Consider how far in advance you will need to call your vet's office to book an appointment.

● ESTABLISHED REPUTATION

Find a veterinarian who graduated from an American Veterinary Medical Association (AVMA)–accredited college and preferably one who sees many companion animals like dogs and cats. Seek reviews and references before committing to one veterinary practice. You can also search for veterinary hospitals in your area that are accredited by the American Animal Hospital Association (AAHA), though many smaller clinics are not certified by this accrediting body.

● CORPORATE VERSUS LOCALLY OPERATED PRACTITIONERS

A number of large corporations have purchased independent clinics throughout the country. A corporate-owned hospital may offer access to a network of veterinary facilities with easily transferable records, while a locally owned hospital may provide more personalized care.

● ABILITY TO SCHEDULE AN INITIAL VISIT WITHIN TWO WEEKS OF BRINGING YOUR NEW DOG HOME

Puppies should not be removed from their mothers until they are 6–7 weeks old, as they will not be weaned until then.

Some states and countries have laws about health standards for the sale of dogs. A veterinarian visit can help mitigate future health concerns and determine the current health of your new dog.

For your first visit to the vet, come prepared with a copy of any previous medical records, a fecal sample, and a list of questions about proper care for your dog using the subsections of this chapter as a guide.

Vaccines

According to the most advanced veterinary science, the section below outlines a routine vaccine timeline recommended for puppies that live in the United States:

- **6–8 WEEKS OLD:** First upper respiratory vaccination. Inoculation against these five diseases is usually administered in one vaccine sometimes collectively referred to as DHPPC: distemper, hepatitis (CAV-2), parvovirus, parainfluenza, and coronavirus.

- **10–11 WEEKS OLD:** Second booster vaccination. Booster for the immune system against DHPPC.

- **14–15 WEEKS OLD:** Third upper respiratory vaccination. Includes DHPPC and leptospirosis, sometimes collectively referred to as DHPPC-L. Inoculation against leptospirosis is safe to administer at 12 weeks of age.

- **18–20 WEEKS OLD:** Fourth upper respiratory vaccination and rabies vaccination.

For dogs 12 months of age or older that live in the United States, annual vaccines are recommended.

- **ANNUAL VACCINES:** Dogs can receive up to five vaccines every year: rabies, DHPPC-L, Bordetella, Lyme disease, and influenza. Most states and counties require rabies vaccinations, and boarding or grooming facilities often require proof of various combinations of these vaccines.

In sum, it is recommended that puppies receive a series of four booster vaccines before they are 20 weeks old. The first vaccine can be given when the puppy is 6–8 weeks old, and each vaccine should be given about 3–4 weeks apart. The rabies vaccine can be administered after the puppy is 16 weeks old. It is recommended that adult dogs receive vaccinations from their veterinarian annually, which may differ slightly based on geographical location, environment, and public health. Your veterinarian may send you reminders when it is time to update your dog's vaccinations. Keep documentation of these vaccines easily accessible, as they may be required by your groomer, boarding facility, etc. See Appendix F: Vaccine Passport for a chart to help track your dog's vaccine status.

Preventatives

An active dog is a happy dog. To help your dog enjoy the outdoors, obtain a prescription to give your dog heartworm, flea, tick, and intestinal parasite (worm) preventatives year-round once they reach about six months old. Cases of dogs diagnosed as heartworm positive or having fleas, intestinal parasites, or ticks are reported in every part of the United States at all times of the year.

These and other diseases can cause serious illness or can be life threatening for your dog, so it is critical to stay up to date on these preventative medications.

Most preventatives should be given on a monthly basis. To ensure doses are not missed, it may be helpful to add reminders to your calendar to administer these medications on the same day each month.

Preventative medicines usually come in the form of oral chews or topical liquid solutions, and they contain medication that prevents these parasites from making your dog ill.

Many products prevent some or all of these conditions and guarantee efficacy. There are many preventative options on the market, and some dogs can be genetically predisposed to sensitivity to certain preventatives. Consult your veterinarian when deciding which medication option is best, as you will need a prescription for one that matches your dog's needs.

Most puppies have intestinal parasites. Puppies should be dewormed by your veterinarian until stool becomes consistent and does not contain parasites. Annual fecal tests are highly recommended for all dogs to check for parasites, and many vets will not sell preventative medications without conducting annual heartworm tests.

Medications

In addition to preventatives, at some point in your dog's life, you will most likely need to administer medications.

Although veterinarians try to mitigate the number of at-home steps, sometimes administering medication orally, topically, or otherwise is necessary to maintain your dog's optimal health. Administration can often be challenging for pet parents.

For oral medications, try covering the pill in peanut butter or cheese to entice your dog to eat and swallow it whole. There are also specially designed treats that help to administer pills by mouth.

If your dog is completely noncompliant with these food-related tricks, watch online tutorial videos on how to "pill" your dog. A pill popper applicator is also a great tool to administer oral medications and can be found online and at pet stores. Certain medications may also be crushed to a powder and added on top of wet or dry dog food.

Make sure to follow proper dosing procedures and any additional medication instructions recommended by your veterinarian.

Spaying and Neutering

If you do not intend to breed or show your dog at competitions, veterinarians recommend having your dog spayed or neutered when they are 5–6 months old.

Pros of spaying and neutering:

- Prevents uterine infections (pyometras) in females and testicular cancer in males, leading to longer life.

- Results in a more gentle, less aggressive disposition.

- Avoids inherent complications of pregnancy for both the mother and the pet owners.

- Reduces the number of dogs that end up in shelters.

Dog breeding is a complex profession that should be managed carefully and ethically. If you are not prepared for this significant financial and time investment, spay or neuter your pet.

Microchipping

For a reasonable cost (about $30 to $60), your dog can be microchipped by a shelter or veterinarian.

A microchip contains a unique identification number that is assigned to you and your pet. About the size of a grain of rice, a microchip is injected under the dog's skin and remains there for the duration of the dog's life. If a microchipped dog gets lost or stolen, a veterinary hospital or animal shelter can use a microchip reader to scan the dog's chip, enter the identification number into the online database, and get in touch with the dog's owner(s). Microchipping is an additional step to help ensure you can reconnect with your dog, as collars and identification tags can be broken, lost, or stolen.

Microchipping is often performed at the time of spaying or neutering while your dog is under anesthesia.

DNA Testing

Get to know your dog down to their DNA! Multiple companies provide affordable direct-to-consumer canine genetic testing. Most tests involve a simple cheek swab, while others require a blood sample. Reliable companies for canine genetic testing include Embark Veterinary, Canine HealthCheck, and Wisdom Panel.

Why test your dog's DNA?

- Learn your dog's breed composition. This test can confirm your breeder's claims or provide interesting insights for adopted, mixed-breed dogs.

- Discover genetic predispositions or traits that may affect your dog's long-term health.

Toxins and Harmful Substances

Many common human foods and household items are toxic to dogs. If your dog ingests any of the following items, call the ASPCA Animal Poison Control Center's 24-hour hotline, (888) 426-4435, then call your veterinarian:

- Alcohol
- Aloe vera
- Avocados
- Caffeine
- Chocolate
- Cooked bones
- Garlic
- Grapes
- Household cleaning supplies and solutions
- Ivy
- Lilies
- Macadamia nuts
- Marijuana and drugs other than those prescribed by your veterinarian
- Nutmeg
- Onions
- Poinsettia plants
- Xylitol and other artificial sweeteners
- Any other non-food item of concern

If you are unsure about whether an item consumed by your dog is dangerous, err on the side of caution and contact Poison Control and/or your veterinarian. As advised by the Veterinary Medical Center of Central New York, be prepared with the following information about your dog's incident with a toxic substance:

- The name of the substance

- The strength of the product, if known (medication, chemical, etc.)

- How much of the substance was consumed

- How much time has passed since consumption occurred

- Age, breed, and approximate weight of your dog

Coprophagia and Other Strange Behavior

Coprophagia is the tendency dogs may have to eat feces. While many over-the-counter products claim they can help prevent dogs from eating their own poop or the poop of other animals, most products do not work. What's the solution? Pick up your dog's poop before they can get to it and keep them away from other animal feces.

Dogs may also eat grass, mulch, dirt, mushrooms, acorns, berries, or other plants, some of which can be harmful. Monitor this behavior closely and ask your veterinarian if you have concerns.

Dental Care

Bad breath and teeth discoloration are signs of dental disease in dogs. Dental disease is common in dogs of all breeds, yet dental hygiene is often overlooked or ignored. Dental disease is especially common (and more severe) in smaller breeds like Yorkshire Terriers and Chihuahuas, or breeds with flatter jaw structures like Boxers and Bulldogs. In most dogs, these issues begin to manifest around three years of age, but it can be prevented or kept from worsening by practicing regular dental hygiene.

PREVENTATIVES AND SOLUTIONS

● Give your dog dental chew sticks. One chew per day is ideal, but check the label to make sure they are appropriately sized for your dog. Dental chews come in various sizes and flavors for both puppies and adult dogs. Select dental chew sticks that are labeled Veterinary Oral Health Council (VOHC) Accepted.

● Medicated dental chews can be prescribed by your veterinarian if your dog has more significant dental issues.

● Brush your dog's teeth. While this is sometimes challenging, watch online tutorials and purchase helpful tools to make teeth brushing easier to do at home, such as flavored enzymatic, pet-friendly toothpastes that can be swallowed.

● Schedule annual dental cleanings for your dog with a veterinarian. Cleanings can be quite costly and require anesthesia, so keeping up with dental hygiene at home year-round can be a good investment. More intensive dental procedures may be avoided with regular care.

Tail Docking, Ear Cropping, and Dewclaw Removal

Tail docking is the surgical shortening or removal of a dog's tail. Some dogs have dewclaws, which are the extra digits on the inside of dogs' legs above the paw pad. If you would like your dog's tail docked, ears cropped, or dewclaws removed, consult your veterinarian. These procedures should be performed before a puppy is seven days old and therefore are usually carried out while the puppy lives with the breeder. Some veterinarians may not perform these procedures, as they can pose ethical concerns.

Other Medical Considerations

- Dogs often swallow small, inedible objects. Veterinarians see cases in which dogs have ingested a wide variety of items including metal coins, plastic toys, rubber watches, wedding rings, baby clothes, human medical pills, and more. Puppies naturally chew on objects to strengthen their teeth, so maintain a dog-proofed house as much as possible. If you suspect your dog ate something indigestible, contact your veterinarian.

- If your dog constantly scoots its rear on the ground, your dog may need its anal glands expressed. This routine procedure can help relieve your dog and can be performed by veterinarians, veterinary technicians, and most groomers.

- If your dog begins to lick its feet a lot, it's likely your pup has allergies. Schedule an appointment with the vet to determine the best course of action.

- If your dog is vomiting, having excessive diarrhea or constipation, consuming water in excess, incessantly coughing or sneezing, or is otherwise expressing abnormal behavior, bring your dog to your veterinarian.

DIET

Dietary considerations for your dog are important but can be overwhelming given the number of options available on the market.

Food Labels and Ingredients

Several reliable dog food brands recommended by veterinarians include:

- Hill's Science Diet
- Royal Canin
- Purina
- Iams

Dog foods from these brands are well tested and formulated for canine health. In general, feed your dog bagged, dry kibble unless otherwise directed by your veterinarian, as dry food supports your dog's dental health.

Diets can vary based on breed and health condition. A quality dog food contains protein (meat or fish), vegetables, grains, and fruits. These contents will provide a good balance of protein, vitamins, and minerals.

The first ingredient on the food label should be the main protein. Current research indicates that grain-free diets are not better for dogs than diets that include grains, so it is important to find foods that do contain some grains. Common grains in dog food include corn, rice, oats, barley, and wheat. Avoid foods with many preservatives. Look on labels and online listings for dog foods that meet the standards of The Association of American Feed Control Officials (AAFCO).

Puppies have different dietary needs than adult dogs. Puppy foods are specially formulated to provide essential nutrients needed during development. Puppies should eat puppy food for at least 12 months, with some dogs remaining on puppy chow for up to 18 months. Feeding adult dog food to a puppy can be detrimental to healthy development. Consult your veterinarian and your breeder or adoption facility for more information.

When transitioning between two types of dog foods, make the transition over a 5- to 7-day period. Transition by mixing part of the current food with part of the new food, incrementally. The AKC recommends the following food transition timeline for most dogs:

DAY	PERCENT NEW DIET	PERCENT OLD DIET
Days 1–2	25%	75%
Days 3–4	50%	50%
Days 5–6	75%	25%
Days 7+	100%	0%

Monitor your dog's stool and behavior during the transitional period between foods. If you notice diarrhea, constipation, vomiting, or other abnormal behavior, consult your veterinarian.

When a dog is sick, bland diets (e.g., boiled chicken and white rice) are often beneficial. Consult your veterinarian for the correct recipes and portion sizes for your pup.

Amounts and Times

In general, adult dogs should be fed twice daily, morning and night, on a consistent schedule. Puppies should be fed more often. Avoid giving table scraps, no matter how much they may beg. Limiting your dog's consumption of human foods prevents bad behavior and helps reduce the risk of long-term health concerns.

When determining how often and how much your dog should eat per day, consult with your veterinarian, as weight, activity level, age, and health conditions should be considered. See Appendix G: Weight Chart and Health Notes for a helpful tracking chart.

Here is a rough rule of thumb for feeding adult dogs that are currently at a healthy weight, but since different food brands have different nutritional compositions, be sure to consider the caloric intake in addition to the measured amount.

WEIGHT	AMOUNT	FREQUENCY
Less than 10 lbs.	⅙–½ cup	2 times per day
10–25 lbs.	Approx. ¾ cup	2 times per day
26–75 lbs.	¾–1 ¼ cup	2 times per day
76–125 lbs.	1 ¼–2 cups	2 times per day
More than 125 lbs.	2–3 cups	2 times per day

Avoid letting your dog exercise immediately before or after eating. Do not feed within 60 minutes before, or within 30 minutes after, exercise. Exercising immediately before or after eating might be linked with bloat (gastric dilatation and volvulus, or GDV), which can be deadly in minutes. Deep-chested dogs are especially predisposed to this condition. Ask your veterinarian how to further mitigate the risk of bloating.

Signs of bloat include:

- Collapsing or inability to stand
- Excessive drooling
- Overall look of distress
- Pacing
- Painful abdomen
- Panting or rapid breathing
- Restlessness

- Retching or unsuccessful attempts to vomit
- Swollen or distended abdomen

If you notice any of these signs, bring your dog to an emergency animal hospital immediately.

Treats

Find a treat that your dog loves as much as you love your favorite dessert! This may take some searching, and the treats your dog likes may change over time. Do not use your dog's regular kibble as treats; make treat time something special so your dog will associate positive behavior with tasty treats.

Practice moderation: Use treats sparingly to reward good behavior. Treats are a powerful training mechanism for your dog. See the Training and Behavior section in this chapter for more guidance.

In addition to specially made dog treats and dental chew treats, other options include peanut butter and cheese. Some dogs even enjoy apples, green beans, and carrots. Explore different options to see which pet-friendly foods your dog likes best.

Find treats that are small, appropriate to the specific diet of your dog, and just a few calories each. Treats should compose no more than 10% of a dog's daily caloric intake, as giving too many treats can cause loose stool and nutritional imbalance. Using smaller treats also allows for more repetition during training sessions.

EXERCISE

Adequate exercise is critical for the health, behavior management, and overall happiness of your dog. Exercise needs vary by breed, so research how much exercise your specific dog needs and make time for it daily. Keep in mind that a tired dog is often a happy dog. See the Diet section above on why you should not exercise your dog immediately before or after meals.

On long walks, especially in warmer months, bring plenty of water to keep your dog well hydrated. Also be aware of pavement temperatures, as many paved surfaces during sunny weather can be significantly hotter than the surrounding air and can severely burn your dog's paws. If the back of your hand cannot stand the heat of the pavement for at least seven seconds, it is too hot for your dog. Walk instead on grassy areas or during a cooler time of day.

Conversely, during colder months, cold pavement, snow, or ice may be too cold for your dog's paws. Winter elements may cause snow and ice to accumulate between your dog's paw pads, which can lead to painful dryness and cracking. De-icers and road salts can also contain toxic chemicals that can burn your dog's paws or expose them to harmful substances. Consider purchasing pet-safe de-icers to use on driveways and sidewalks. Purchasing booties is another solution to help protect your dog's paws when walking in winter weather conditions.

Leashes and Harnesses

When walking your dog, be sure to secure a well-fitted collar or harness and attach a sturdy leather or nylon leash. When properly fitted, you should be able to place two fingers between the collar or harness strap and your dog's neck or body to confirm that the collar is not to too tight or too loose. Retractable leashes are not recommended, as they can be hazardous and can promote pulling behavior.

Opinions and training methods vary as to whether choke collars and electric collars are appropriate, but first try using a standard or martingale-style collar that limits the amount of tightening pressure that can be inflicted around the dog's neck. Many dogs have a natural pull instinct that is triggered when they feel pressure in the opposite direction. Excessive pulling of a leash resulting in collar pressure can cause severe and lasting damage to your dog's neck and throat. If it is difficult to walk your dog without tension on the leash and pulling behavior, then seek training and consider switching to a no-pull harness that attaches around the chest and back.

Tags

Once you select the perfect collar or harness, be sure to securely attach identification and rabies tags. Your veterinarian will provide rabies tags at the time of vaccine administration. Customized ID tags can be ordered online or through your local pet supply store. The tags should contain the dog's name and the owner's name, home address, and at least one phone number. You may also choose to note if your dog is microchipped to help expedite the scanning process if your dog is ever lost.

Depending on your budget, you can monitor your dog's location and exercise behavior by purchasing tags and collars with GPS tracking in addition to exercise and sleep tracking. Some GPS collars allow you to set multiple perimeters for different locations where you frequently bring your dog.

Potty Bags

Affix a potty bag dispenser to your leash so you have them handy every time you go for a walk. Always clean up after your pet when walking in public places. Your local park, if dog-friendly, may also have signposts that offer free potty bags and trash bins.

Toys

Toys, like exercise, are important for your dog's mental development and overall happiness. Every dog has different preferences when it comes to toys, and there are countless options to buy, from standard fetch and tug-of-war toys to more complex puzzle games. So experiment, have fun, and see what your pup likes best. Double check that any toy you select is an appropriate size for your dog and is not a choking hazard.

Rawhide toys should be monitored because they can become a choking hazard when chewed to tiny bits. Similarly, tennis balls make good fetch toys but can also be hazardous for teeth. Toys that are too hard can put your dog at risk for tooth breakage, so look for toys that have some flexibility or give. Your dog may chew apart soft squeak toys to locate the source of the noise, so monitor them to make sure the squeaker or other small pieces do not pose a choking risk.

Rotate the toys available to your dog to keep playtime interesting and fun.

GROOMING

Depending on your dog's coat and affinity for getting dirty, it is helpful to have a selection of grooming and cleaning supplies on hand. Professional groomers are also a great option depending on your budget.

Brushing

Find a brush that is appropriate for your dog's coat. A best practice is to brush your dog's coat at least every other day—regardless of coat type or length—to remove hair, distribute natural oils, and provide you with an opportunity to examine your dog for any skin wounds, growths, or sensitivities. For thick-coated dogs, you may want to purchase a de-shedding brush designed to remove the loose undercoat without damaging the topcoat.

Nail Trimming

Nail trimming is a grooming activity many dogs simply do not like, but it is a necessary part of maintaining good health. Keeping your dog's nails trimmed helps prevent chipping, splintering, and other painful conditions. When your dog's nails become long enough to hear audible clicking when they walk on hard surfaces, it is time to clip—likely about once every two weeks.

You may choose to trim your dog's nails at home with designated clippers, or you may prefer to ask your vet or groomer to trim them periodically. Owners often find it challenging to restrain their dog during this process, and the risk of hitting blood vessels and causing pain or bleeding is high when a dog fidgets. As such, many owners decide to outsource this task. If you opt to trim at home, a clever (and comical) technique can be found online that involves wrapping plastic wrap around your forehead and smearing peanut butter on the plastic wrap to keep your dog distracted while you clip.

Bathing

Bathing your dog can be a chaotic experience, but washing is essential to keep its coat healthy, clean, and smelling good. Find a shampoo/conditioner that is appropriate for your dog's coat. A good rule of thumb is to bathe your dog about once every four weeks, or as needed. Bathing can be accomplished at home in a standard bathtub, outside in a plastic tub or kiddie pool, or you may opt to use a grooming facility. Some dog groomers offer do-it-yourself bathing stations, or you can hire a professional groomer to bathe and brush your dog.

Many dogs will not initially love the experience of bath time, but if approached thoughtfully, they may build positive associations with the experience over time. Rewarding your dog with treats or a favorite snack throughout the washing process can improve their disposition. You can find online resources and tutorial videos demonstrating diversion techniques such as applying peanut butter to the bath tile to distract your dog while you wash them in the tub. Get creative and try to make bathing a fun and exciting experience for your pooch.

TRAINING AND BEHAVIOR

Please note that this is not a training book. There are simply too many techniques and dog training theories to review in this short book. To begin the process, research the different training methods and find an accredited course or trainer near you that aligns with your preferred approach. See Appendix A: Additional Resources for recommended training resources.

Training Theories and Resources

It is important to recognize that nearly all dogs are trainable. Dogs are bred to be task-oriented and want to be challenged, trained, and rewarded. While it can be a tedious and often frustrating process, if you consistently follow the coaching and methodology of an accredited program, you are highly likely to cultivate a responsive, well-trained, and happy dog.

Fundamentally, all training programs are based on the same premise: Dogs are prediction machines! They are constantly anticipating what will happen next based upon their past experiences. Using patterns in their environment as cues, they predict the positive or negative reinforcement they think will happen next and respond accordingly. In other words, if something good happens in the eyes of the dog and they receive a treat, they will likely associate that reward with the action that happened immediately beforehand. Over time, they will seek to repeat the same behavior that led to that reward.

Note that the behavior the dog associates with the reward may not be the exact same behavior you are trying to reinforce. For example, you might reward your dog for stopping a behavior that you deem as negative (e.g., jumping up on people), yet they may associate the treat with the jumping behavior rather than the stopping of that same action. So, it is important to isolate specific, individual behaviors and associate them with rewards.

The better the positive reward (like a tasty treat) and the more often it is repeated, the stronger the association will become for your dog. Prioritize positive reinforcement during training sessions, be consistent, and pick special treats that your dog absolutely loves.

Inversely, when something bad happens in the eyes of the dog, or when something good is taken away, your dog will generally avoid the behavior that led to the negative outcome. Whether positive or negative, regular repetition of the cue, routine, and reward is key to ingraining that pattern in your dog's brain.

In addition, dogs do not tend to generalize behaviors well across different contexts, so training in different environments with different levels of distraction is important. Remember, consistency of habits and routines is critical in training, as your dog constantly forms expectations of future events based on pattern recognition from past events. They typically do not understand the "why" behind good or bad actions; they simply remember whether they are associated with good or bad outcomes.

Behavioral Problems and Expectations

Dogs are likely to exhibit at least a few common behavioral problems, including aggressive behavior, barking, begging, biting, chewing, digging, humping, ignoring commands, jumping, leash pulling, potty accidents, separation anxiety, and whining. None of these behaviors should be insurmountable with ample training and dedication.

It may be useful to view these behaviors as learning opportunities for you as the dog's trainer rather than acting out in anger or frustration toward the dog. Remember, your dog only knows how to communicate to you through their actions. It is your responsibility as a dog owner to try to make sense of that communication and act accordingly.

Potty Training

Potty training your new dog is another part of the training process. With enough consistency and positive reinforcement over time, they will learn to potty in the proper place. That said, most dogs will occasionally have an accident in the house, often in dark or secluded areas that are not highly trafficked. These messes can be caused by anxiety, a break from routine, illness, or simply needing relief and not having the opportunity to go outside.

Indoor "potty pads" or specially designed training papers offer an alternative way for dogs to relieve themselves without having to go outside. Though it is possible to use newspapers as a training paper option, they often are not very absorbent and may result in tracking urine throughout in the house. The scent of residual urine may then serve as an invitation for the dog to return to the same unwanted spot to potty in the future.

Dogs tend to avoid going to the bathroom in the same place where they sleep, so they will hold their bladder for as long as possible rather than soiling their crate or sleeping area. That said, dogs, like people, can only hold their bladders for so long before they will have to go. In general, puppies can hold their bladder for one hour for every month of age, plus one. So, a three-month-old puppy can likely hold their bladder for about four hours. That said, you should try to take them out to potty more often than this to avoid accidents. A healthy adult dog can go 10–12 hours without peeing, but they should typically be let outside at least once every eight hours, or 3–5 times per day. A senior dog will need to be let out progressively more often. Always stay attuned to your dog's signals and body language that tell you they may need some relief.

Teething

Puppies normally lose their baby teeth between 3–6 weeks of age. By six weeks old, the adult teeth become visible, and around the six-month mark, a puppy should have all of their adult teeth. Puppies will bite...a lot. Chewing is a natural instinct for dogs that can help clean teeth and relieve anxiety.

Why puppies chew:

- Though varied by breed, puppies use their mouth to understand and feel their surroundings as they mature.

- Chewing is also a method to ease discomfort brought about by growing and strengthening adult teeth.

To help your puppy stop chewing on your own personal items, provide them with specifically designed toys that help with teething. Do not leave puppies unsupervised around objects that they should not chew.

Socialization and Dog–Dog Introductions

When introducing your dog to a new dog, it is recommended to hold the initial meeting in a neutral location where neither dog will feel territorial. Ensure both owners are present and both dogs are on leashes. Keep the leashes loose and maintain a calm, positive demeanor and tone of voice. Let the two dogs gradually smell each other and allow them to meet briefly, paying close attention for hostile or aggressive body language. As the meeting progresses, reward both dogs with positive feedback, treats, and praise, and separate them periodically to provide a break.

It is common for dogs to engage in a brief tussle upon first meeting. This behavior is normal and often does not result in injury, but monitor the interactions closely to ensure they do not extend for more than a few seconds or become violent. Be prepared to distract the dogs with a loud noise (e.g., banging pots) or a nonviolent pattern interrupt (e.g., splashing with water) if behavior becomes too rough. Never attempt to separate a dog fight with your hands. If your dog is consistently uncomfortable or aggressive when meeting new dogs, seek the help of a professional trainer.

If your new dog is adopted into a home with existing dogs, cats, or other pets, similar guidelines apply. Initial meetings should be controlled and in a neutral place. Make the first several visits among new and existing pets short, gradually increasing exposure as the pets become more familiar with one another. It is common for existing pets to be unwelcoming to a newly introduced dog in the home, especially if the new dog is permitted to encroach onto a space generally reserved for the existing pet. It may take some time and effort to ensure that they respect each other's space, food, toys, and privacy, and over time with gradually increased exposure, they will become more friendly and cohabitate peacefully.

LEAVING YOUR DOG

Leaving town without your dog can be a stressful experience for both the dog and owner. Dogs often experience separation anxiety when left home alone or at a boarding facility. This anxiety can manifest in unwanted behaviors including escape attempts, excessive barking, destructive behavior, potty accidents, or increased physiological responses (e.g., drooling, heavy breathing, increased heart rate, or panting). Though some amount of separation anxiety may be unavoidable, the symptoms can be mitigated by providing sufficient exercise before leaving your dog. Additionally, reserve a special treat (e.g., puzzle treat, licking mat, or KONG toy filled with frozen peanut butter) to give your dog before departing so they can form a positive rather than negative association with your absence. Toys that require repeated licking action can help relieve stress in dogs and can be an invaluable asset in any stress-inducing situation. If separation anxiety continues without improvement, seek a qualified trainer to work with you and your dog.

Boarding

A few weeks before a trip, identify several local pet boarding facilities that are highly reviewed and where you feel comfortable leaving your pup. Some veterinary clinics also offer boarding services, which can be a good option for older dogs or dogs that need special oversight.

Ask to tour the facility and assess the professionalism, knowledge, and experience of the staff. Observe for cleanliness and ask about daily procedures and emergency protocols. The kennel may require a meet-and-greet prior to the initial overnight visit to see how your dog interacts with other dogs, so do not wait until the last minute to find a facility. Some boarding facilities may also require a physical exam to be completed on-site, so it is critical to schedule overnight stays with enough lead time.

Prepare up-to-date copies of all vaccination and medical records to provide to the boarding facility before your dog's first visit.

Boarding services can vary widely in cost, from $15 to well over $50 daily, and à la carte add-on services may be available for a resort-like experience.

Daycare

Depending on your day-to-day schedule, you may want to enroll your dog in daycare. Daycare establishments often provide your dog with play time, socialization with other dogs, and nap opportunities. Many dog daycare facilities provide a pickup and drop-off service, as well as onsite training classes. Daycare may be a good option if your schedule does not permit enough time to regularly exercise your dog.

Daycare options can vary widely in cost, from $20 to $40+ per day. Some daycares offer multiday packages or monthly memberships at discounted daily prices.

Dog Walkers

As an alternative to daycare, you may consider finding a local dog walker by searching online, asking your vet or boarding facility, posting a classified ad (e.g., Craigslist or Nextdoor), or asking for recommendations from friends in your local community. Some online platforms specifically connect dog owners with pet sitters and dog walkers.

The cost for dog walking typically ranges from $15 to $30 per walk.

TRAVELING WITH YOUR DOG

Traveling with a canine companion requires some extra considerations but can be fun and well worth the effort.

Flying

Flying with your dog, while possible, can be administratively challenging and costly, with many airlines requiring a separate ticket for your pup. Be sure to leave ample time beforehand to prepare the required documents and receive approval. Only official service dogs and dogs meeting the airline's size and weight criteria are allowed to fly with owners in the main cabin of an airplane. Most airlines will allow larger dogs to be transported in cargo as long as the carrier meets their criteria for rigidity and ventilation. Since flying is a departure from their normal routine, dogs may also exhibit anxious or nervous behaviors before, during, or after flying.

Key steps to take before flying with your dog:

- Check with your airline carrier to determine their regulations regarding flying with animals.

- Check the United States Department of Agriculture (USDA) website to find domestic and international travel requirements and paperwork.

- Schedule a pre-flight exam with your veterinarian to confirm that your dog is healthy enough to make the trip. Some veterinarians may prescribe antianxiety medication, if needed. Collect any necessary records or signatures on required paperwork.

- When planning your trip, consider identifying an animal hospital in your destination city in case of an emergency.

- Pack sufficient dog food, portable water bowls, treats, and prescribed medications.

Driving

Taking your dog on a road trip can be a wonderful bonding experience, but it has its limitations, too. Check state and local laws for requirements on restraining dogs in a moving vehicle, as states have differing levels of regulations. Dog seat belts and car kennel options help keep your dog safe in the car. Never leave your dog unrestrained in a car, as they could jump out or fall from the vehicle during quick stops, turns, or crashes. Open car windows need to be closely monitored to ensure your dog cannot fit through. Do not travel with your dog unrestrained in the bed of a pickup truck, as many terrible injuries and pet deaths occur from dogs jumping from truck-beds—all of which could be prevented.

Never leave your dog unattended in a parked car for any amount of time, regardless of weather conditions. Even with the windows slightly open, the internal temperature of your vehicle will become far more extreme than the outside temperature within a matter of minutes. The lack of circulating air can unintentionally lead to devastating outcomes for your pet.

RESOURCES AND FURTHER READING

Folk will know how large your soul
is by the way you treat a dog.

—CHARLES F. DORAN

We hope you enjoyed this book and found the information as useful as we have in raising our own pups. May this be just the beginning of a lifetime of learning and love for your incredible canine companions.

The following section contains additional resources and references that may further assist you as you bring a new dog into your home.

Thank you for reading, and happy tails!

ADDITIONAL RESOURCES

GENERAL RESOURCES

Air Travel Requirements:
- www.aphis.usda.gov/aphis/pet-travel

Budgeting for a Dog:
- www.k9ofmine.com/how-to-budget-for-dog/
- https://www.rover.com/blog/cost-of-owning-a-dog/

Comprehensive Breed List and Tool for Comparing Breed Attributes:
- www.akc.org/dog-breeds/

Dog Car Restraints Interactive U.S. Map:
- news.orvis.com/dogs/does-your-state-require-dogs-be-harnessed-in-the-car

Pet Insurance Overview:
- www.moneyunder30.com/pet-insurance

Pros and Cons of Invisible Fences:

- https://vcahospitals.com/know-your-pet/the-pros-and-cons-of-invisible-fences-for-dogs

TRAINING RESOURCES

Common Behavioral Problems in Dogs:

- https://pets.webmd.com/dogs/ss/slideshow-behavioral-problems-in-dogs
- https://www.aspca.org/pet-care/dog-care/common-dog-behavior-issues

How Long Dogs Can Hold Their Bladder:

- https://blog.homesalive.ca/dog-blog/how-long-can-dogs-hold-their-pee

Introducing Dogs to Each Other:

- https://resources.bestfriends.org/article/introducing-dogs-each-other

Popular Dog Training Methods:

- https://dogtime.com/reference/dog-training/50743-7-popular-dog-training-methods

Separation Anxiety Overview:

- https://www.akc.org/expert-advice/training/dog-separation-anxiety-how-to-stop/

The 3/3/3 Rule:

- https://www.rescuedogs101.com/bringing-new-dog-home-3-3-3-rule/#3-3-3-rule

SERVICE DOGS

U.S. Service Animal Registry:

- https://usserviceanimalregistrar.org/ada-list-of-disabilities/?utm_term=&gclid=CjwKCAiAwKyNBh BfEiwA_mrUMoaMJ2en-Dkenl3FKAodKQlwc5Bj2l WuRlwcxrtKNUWd2mU8xSJdERoC4IgQAvD_BwE

More Information on Service Dogs:

- https://www.akc.org/expert-advice/training/service-dog-training-101/

- https://www.akc.org/expert-advice/training/service-working-therapy-emotional-support-dogs/

TEMPERAMENT ASSESSMENT

A number of assessment tools evaluate the temperament and personality traits of dogs. Some proven methods may be helpful as you evaluate a dog prior to adoption. Ask your local shelter or breeder if they have already conducted or will help you conduct any of these or similar temperament assessments.

The following list of questions adapted from the Rescue Dogs 101 website is a great starting point to assess a dog for possible adoption.

DOG ADOPTION INTERVIEW QUESTIONS

- How did the dog come to be in the shelter or foster home?

- How long has the dog been in the shelter or foster home?

- Why was he surrendered?

- Where does he sleep at night?

- Has he been to a groomer before? How did it go?

- Does he allow you to trim his nails, clean his ears, and/or give him a bath?

Health Questions

- Has the dog had a general wellness exam by a veterinarian? When? Does he have any known medical issues?

- Is the dog neutered or spayed?

- Is he current on all vaccines? (If you adopt him, make sure to get copies of all vet records.)

- Is he current on heartworm and flea/tick preventatives?

- Has he had a SNAP 4 Dx test? (A SNAP 4 Dx test is a blood test that is run by a vet. While not required, it provides valuable information. The test is a screening process for six vector-borne diseases: Heartworm, Lyme, *Ehrlichia canis*, *Ehrlichia ewingii*, *Anaplasma phagocytophilum* and *Anaplasma platys*.)

- Does he have a microchip?

- Does he have any allergies?

- Check the dog's eyes and ears for yourself. Are the eyes clear of discharge, and are the inside of the ears clean?

Potty Training Questions

- Is the dog potty trained?

- Does he use any signals to ask to go outside?

- How often does he go outside?

Energy Level Questions

- How much exercise does this dog need?

- What is his typical energy level like?

- How many times a day does he need to be walked, and for how long?

- Does he relax and lie down when you are ready to stop playing?

- What are his favorite activities (e.g., playing fetch, swimming, frisbee, walking, or running)?

- Would he be a good dog for going on hikes or running?

Crate Training Questions

- Is the dog crate trained?

- If he's not crate trained, do you leave him loose when you're not home? If so, how does he do? Any mischievous behavior?

- How does he act in a crate? Is he calm or anxious? Does he bark?

- How do you think he does when left alone?

Behavior Questions

- Does the dog have any resource-guarding issues with food, toys, or anything else?

- Is he independent or dependent? Is he unsure or shy?

- Does he show any signs of separation anxiety?

- Does he bark excessively when left alone?

- How long can he be left home alone?

- Does he have any fears (e.g., thunderstorms or loud noises)?

- Does he chew things such as kids' toys, furniture, or shoes?

- Does he like to play with other dogs?

- Is this dog friendly around other dogs? How does he act when he meets new dogs, on leash and off leash?

- Ask to see him interact with another dog.

- Have you ever taken him to a dog park? How did it go?

- If you have a cat, has he been around a cat before? How does he act around cats?

- Is there anything that brings out fear or aggression (like bikers, strangers, men, etc.)?

- How does he act around strangers? Is he scared, shy, aggressive, or friendly when meeting new people?

- Is the dog child-friendly? Has he been around kids? How old were the kids? How does he act around them?

- Has he ever nipped, bit, or attacked anyone?

- Do you consider him a vocal dog? What makes the dog bark? Does he bark when left alone, at the doorbell, or at people or dogs on walks?

- How is he in the car? Is he calm, overly excited, or scared of the car?

Training Questions
- Has the dog had any formal training for behavior, obedience, hunting, agility, etc.?

- What commands does he know? (Ask for specific words or hand signals used; this will help you understand how to interact with the dog if you adopt him.)

- What type of training tools have been used on him (like an electric collar, prong collar, etc.)?

- How does he walk on a leash? Does he walk with a flat collar, harness, prong collar, martingale-style collar, or any other tools?

- Does he pull or lunge at other dogs, people, cars, or bikes?

- Can I take him for a short walk? (If you have another dog, ask if you can walk the two dogs together.)

- Does he have any known behavioral issues?

- Is he food motivated?

- What type of discipline works with him? A firm no, a leash correction, redirection, or time-out?

(**SOURCE:** www.rescuedogs101.com/53-questionsask-adopting-dog)

ADDITIONAL TEMPERAMENT ASSESSMENT TOOLS

American Kennel Club (AKC) Temperament Test:
- https://www.akc.org/akctemptest/

Behavior and Personality Assessment in Dogs (BPH) developed by the Swedish Kennel Club (SKK):
- https://www.skk.se/globalassets/dokument/ uppfodning/broschyrer/bph-behavior-and- personality-assessment-a66.pdf

Behavior Assessment Reactivity Checklist (B.A.R.C.):
- https://boundangels.org/barc/

Match-Up II by the Animal Rescue League of Boston (ARL):
- https://www.arlboston.org/services/match-up/

Safety Assessment for Evaluating Rehoming (SAFER) by the American Society for the Prevention of Cruelty to Animals (ASPCA):
- https://aspcapro.org/sites/default/files/safer- guide-and-forms.pdf

BUDGETING WORKSHEET

ONE-TIME EXPENSES	BUDGET	ACTUAL
Adoption Fees	$_____	$_____
Crate/Bed	$_____	$_____
Fence/Pen	$_____	$_____
Leash/Collar/Harness	$_____	$_____
Grooming Supplies	$_____	$_____
Toys	$_____	$_____
Training Materials/ Courses	$_____	$_____
Vet Screening/Vaccinations	$_____	$_____
Spaying/ Neutering/Microchipping	$_____	$_____
Other:		
_____	$_____	$_____
_____	$_____	$_____
Total One-Time Expenses	$_____	$_____

MONTHLY EXPENSES	BUDGET	ACTUAL
Food	$_____	$_____
Treats	$_____	$_____
Potty Bags	$_____	$_____
Medications	$_____	$_____
Grooming/Bathing	$_____	$_____
Veterinary Visits (semi-annual)	$_____	$_____
Pet Insurance	$_____	$_____
Travel	$_____	$_____
Boarding/Daycare	$_____	$_____
Other:		
_____	$_____	$_____
Total Monthly Expenses	$_____	$_____

APPENDIX D

CONTACT INFORMATION

Primary Veterinarian

Name:_____

Phone:_____

Email:_____

Address:_____

Notes:_____

24/7 Veterinary Clinic

Name:_____

Phone:_____

Email:_____

Address:_____

Notes:_____

Animal Poison Control Center's 24-Hour Hotline
Phone: **(888) 426-4435**

Boarding Facility

Name: _____

Phone: _____

Email: _____

Address: _____

Notes: _____

Grooming Facility

Name: _____

Phone: _____

Email: _____

Address: _____

Notes: _____

Other

Name: _____

Phone: _____

Email: _____

Address: _____

Notes: _____

PET ALERT

For peace of mind, it is advised to post a pet alert notice like the one below in a visible place on or near your front door. This signage can alert first responders to rescue your pet(s) in an emergency like a fire or natural disaster. These decals can be purchased at your local pet supply store, online, or can be ordered for free by registering with the American Society for the Prevention of Cruelty to Animals (ASPCA).

(Adapted from https://secure.aspca.org/take-action/pet-safety-pack)

VACCINE PASSPORT

VACCINE	DATE ADMINISTERED	NOTES
1st Puppy Vaccine: DHPPC Ideal Age Range: 6–8 weeks old		
2nd Puppy Booster: DHPPC Ideal Age Range: 10–11 weeks old		
3rd Puppy Booster: DHPP-L Ideal Age Range: 14–15 weeks old		
4th Puppy Booster: DHPP-L Ideal Age Range: 18–20 weeks old		

Rabies Vaccine Ideal Age Range: Over 16 weeks old		

WEIGHT CHART AND HEALTH NOTES

DATE OF VETERINARY VISIT	WEIGHT	HEALTH NOTES

DATE OF VETERINARY VISIT	WEIGHT	HEALTH NOTES

DATE OF VETERINARY VISIT	WEIGHT	HEALTH NOTES

BIBLIOGRAPHY

Service, Therapy, Emotional Support, and Working Dogs:

AMS Printing. n.d. "Pet Window Decal: Pet Alert, Dog Fire Rescue Label." Accessed May 1, 2023. https://www.amsprinting.com/products/emergency-pet-rescue-labels/pet-window-decal-pet-alert-dog-fire-rescue-label.

Karetnick, Jen. 2022. "Service Dog 101–Everything You Need to Know." American Kennel Club. May 20, 2022. https://www.akc.org/expert-advice/training/service-dog-training-101/.

Reisen, Jan. 2021. "Service Dogs, Working Dogs, Therapy Dogs, Emotional Support Dogs: What's the Difference?" American Kennel Club. February 24, 2021. https://www.akc.org/expert-advice/training/service-working-therapy-emotional-support-dogs/.

US Service Animal Registrar. n.d. "ADA List of Disabilities to Qualify for a Service Dog." Accessed May 1, 2023. https://usserviceanimalregistrar.org/ada-list-of-disabilities/.

The Search:

AKC Staff. 2020. "The 7 AKC Dog Breed Groups Explained." American Kennel Club. January 29, 2020. https://www.akc.org/expert-advice/lifestyle/7-akc-dog-breed-groups-explained/.

American Kennel Club. n.d. "AKC Breeder Referral Search." Accessed May 1, 2023. https://webapps.akc.org/breeder-referral/#/search.

American Kennel Club. n.d. "Dog Breeds." Accessed May 1, 2023. https://www.akc.org/dog-breeds/.

Cushing, Mark. 2019. "The Dog Shortage Is Real." Today's Veterinary Business. December 1, 2019. https://todaysveterinarybusiness.com/the-dog-shortage-is-real/.

Hansen, Sarah. 2019. "Adoption from Shelter vs. Buying from a Breeder: What's Best for You?" Labrador Training HQ. October 14, 2019. https://www.labradortraininghq.com/labrador-puppies/adoption-vs-breeder-whats-best/.

James, John. 2022. "Pet Allergy." Asthma and Allergy Foundation of America. June 2022. https://www.aafa.org/pet-dog-cat-allergies/.

Mejia, Carolina. 2022. "The Pros and Cons of Adopting a Dog." PetHelpful. March 3, 2023. https://pethelpful.com/dogs/5-Pros-And-5-Cons-of-Adopting-a-Dog.

Budgeting:

The Dog People. n.d. "How much does it cost to be a dog parent?" Accessed May 1, 2023. https://www.rover.com/blog/cost-of-owning-a-dog/.

Muller, Chris. 2023. "The Annual Cost of Pet Ownership: Can You Afford a Furry Friend?" Money Under 30. Accessed January 26, 2023. https://www.moneyunder30.com/the-true-cost-of-pet-ownership.

Tak, Claire. 2019. "Pet Fees: What to Expect in a Tenant Pet Agreement." Apartment Guide. September 6, 2019. https://www.apartmentguide.com/blog/pet-fees-what-to-expect/.

Van Pelt, Kate. 2023. "Should You Buy a Pet Insurance 'Pawlicy'? – When Is Insurance For Your Pet Worth It." Money Under 30. Accessed April 12, 2023. https://www.moneyunder30.com/pet-insurance.

Preparing the House:

Buzhardt, Lynn. n.d. "The Pros and Cons of Invisible Fences for Dogs." VCA Animal Hospitals. Accessed May 1, 2023. https://vcahospitals.com/know-your-pet/the-pros-and-cons-of-invisible-fences-for-dogs.

Crocetti, Rachel. 2019. "How Do You Prepare to Bring a New Dog Home?" BARK Post. May 12, 2019. https://barkpost.com/life/prepare-home-for-dog/.

Stoica, Ovidiu. 2022. "How to Prepare Your Household for a New Dog." wikiHow. February 21, 2022. https://www.wikihow.com/Prepare-Your-Household-for-a-New-Dog.

Shelter:
Rescue Dogs 101. n.d. "The 3-3-3 rule and bringing home a rescue dog." Accessed May 1, 2023. https://www.rescuedogs101.com/bringing-new-dog-home-3-3-3-rule/#3-3-3-rule.

Medical:
ASPCA. n.d. "Animal Poison Control." Accessed May 1, 2023. https://www.aspca.org/pet-care/animal-poison-control.

Hiscox, Lorraine, and Jan Bellows. n.d. "Dental Disease in Dogs." VCA Animal Hospitals. Accessed May 1, 2023. https://vcahospitals.com/know-your-pet/dental-disease-in-dogs.

Veterinary Medical Center of Central New York. n.d. "Gastric Dilatation-Volvulus (Bloat)." Accessed May 1, 2023. https://www.vmccny.com/gastric-dilatationvolvulus-bloat.

Veterinary Medical Center of Central New York. n.d. "Poisons and Toxins." Accessed May 1, 2023. https://www.vmccny.com/poisoning-and-toxins.

Weddington Animal Hospital. n.d. "10 Houseplants That Are Dangerous for Your Dog." Accessed May 1, 2023. https://www.weddingtonanimalhospital.com/10-houseplants-that-are-dangerous-for-your-dog/.

Diet:

AKC Staff. 2022. "How to Switch & Transition Dog Foods." American Kennel Club. March 2, 2022. https://www.akc.org/expert-advice/nutrition/right-way-switch-dog-foods/.

ASPCA. 2020. "Grain-Free Pet Food: Helpful or Harmful Diet?" February 27, 2020. https://www.aspca.org/news/grain-free-pet-food-helpful-or-harmful-diet.

Godio, Mili. 2022. "How to buy the best dog treats, according to veterinarians." NBC News, NBCUniversal News Group. July 22, 2020. https://www.nbcnews.com/select/shopping/best-dog-treats-ncna1234429.

Purina. n.d. "Dog Feeding Chart: How Much Should I Feed My Dog?" Accessed May 1, 2023. https://www.purina.com/articles/dog/feeding/how-much-should-i-feed-my-dog.

Exercise:

FOUR PAWS International. 2019. "Hot Asphalt: A Danger to Your Dog's Paws." June 28, 2019. https://www.four-paws.org/our-stories/publications-guides/hot-asphalt-a-danger-to-your-dogs-paws.

The Humane Society of the United States. n.d. "How to pick the best and safest dog toy." Accessed May 1, 2023. https://www.humanesociety.org/resources/safe-dog-toys.

Pup Life. n.d. "How to Choose the Right Dog Toys For Your Pet." Accessed May 1, 2023. https://www.puplife.com/pages/choosing-the-right-dog-toys-for-your-pet.

Stuart, Annie. 2021. "Rawhide: Good or Bad for Your Dog?" Fetch, WebMD. May 8, 2021. https://pets.webmd.com/dogs/rawhide-good-or-bad-for-your-dog#1.

Grooming:

Animal Humane Society. n.d. "Dog grooming tips to keep your pet looking (and feeling) their best." Accessed May 1, 2023. https://www.animalhumanesociety.org/resource/dog-grooming-tips-keep-your-pet-looking-and-feeling-their-best.

Training and Behavior:

ASPCA. n.d. "Common Dog Behavior Issues." Accessed May 1, 2023. https://www.aspca.org/pet-care/dog-care/common-dog-behavior-issues.

Best Friends. n.d. "Introducing Dogs to Each Other." Accessed May 1, 2023. https://resources.bestfriends.org/article/introducing-dogs-each-other.

Clark, Mike. n.d. "7 Most Popular Dog Training Methods." DogTime Accessed May 1, 2023. https://dogtime.

com/reference/dog-training/50743-7-popular-dog-training-methods.

Janisse, Krystn. 2021. "How Long Can Dogs Hold Their Pee? How Long Can Puppy Hold Pee?" Homes Alive Pets. April 24, 2021. https://blog.homesalive.ca/dog-blog/how-long-can-dogs-hold-their-pee.

WedMD Editorial Contributors. 2021. "Dog Training: Obedience Training for Dogs." Fetch, WebMD. June 30, 2021. https://pets.webmd.com/dogs/guide/dog-training-obedience-training-for-dogs.

Williams, Krista, and Richard Lerner. n.d. "Teeth, Teething and Chewing in Puppies." VCA Animal Hospitals. Accessed May 1, 2023. https://vcahospitals.com/know-your-pet/teeth-teething-and-chewing-in-puppies.

Leaving Your Dog:
Canine Comfort Dog Daycare & Boarding. n.d. "Dog Daycare at Canine Comfort." Accessed May 1, 2023. http://www.caninecomfortdaycare.com/dog-daycare-at-canine-comfort/.

Traveling with Your Dog:
GoPetFriendly. 2021. "Is It Illegal to Leave Your Pet Alone in the Car?" January 5, 2021. https://www.go-petfriendly.com/blog/is-it-illegal-to-leave-your-pet-alone-in-the-car/.

Orvis Staff. 2021. "Does Your State Require Dogs Be Harnessed in the Car?" Orvis News. July 30, 2021. https://news.orvis.com/dogs/does-your-state-require-dogs-be-harnessed-in-the-car.

USDA Animal and Plant Health Inspection Service. 2022. "APHIS Pet Travel." August 11, 2022. https://www.aphis.usda.gov/aphis/pet-travel.

Appendix B: Temperament Assessment:
Rescue Dogs 101. n.d. "53 Questions You MUST Ask a Rescue BEFORE Adopting a Dog." Accessed May 1, 2023. https://www.rescuedogs101.com/53-questions-ask-adopting-dog/

INDEX

FEEDBACK

What are we missing in this handbook? Are there topics that you wish had been discussed and are not currently included in the book? We would love to hear from you, and we welcome your feedback to help make future versions of this book as useful as possible.

Connect with us on social media or email us at **info@ essentialdogownersguide.com**. We always reply.

You can find links to social media and more on our website: **essentialdogownersguide.com**

Send pictures of your dog with this book via email or social media and we may post them to our website and social media channels.

THANK YOU FOR YOUR SUPPORT!

ABOUT THE AUTHORS

Reed and Evan Milnor are dog-obsessed brothers from Alton, Illinois, a small suburb outside of St. Louis, Missouri, where they grew up with their family's lovable chocolate Labrador Charlie Gunner and mixed-breed rescue pup Sophie Odelette. In early 2021, Reed and Evan were inspired to write this book to help consolidate and share their learnings about proper dog care.

Reed has worked at multiple veterinary clinics, where he learned the clinical side of animal care. He also helped assemble the world's largest repository of dog genetic and health data at a canine genetic research startup organization. Reed is currently in the Doctor of Veterinary Medicine program at the Cornell University College of Veterinary Medicine.

Evan has had a deep love for nature, animals, and the outdoors since childhood and is currently the owner of a dog training company based in St. Louis, Missouri. He was inspired to co-author this book after he and his wife adopted a three-year-old Siberian Husky-Samoyed mix named Ullr and quickly realized how many elements of dog care they wish they had known prior to adoption.

In the ensuing months, nearly every conversation amongst family and friends turned to discussing dog ownership, sharing photos, and asking questions about proper canine care. Those questions regularly sent Reed and Evan to books, articles, and the internet to search for expert advice. They soon realized that a concise but thorough handbook would be helpful for new dog owners. Reed and Evan sincerely hope that this guidebook is a helpful resource for many generations of dog owners to come.

BOOK ORDERS

To order more copies of this book for fellow dog parents, a vet's office, your local shelter, or more, please visit our website:

essentialdogownersguide.com

THANK YOU FOR READING!

Made in the USA
Las Vegas, NV
16 January 2025

16535602R00075